MILLFI

Library an

This book m

before the latest date marked below

WITHDRAWN

About the Author

Mike Gershon is known in the United Kingdom and beyond as an expert educationalist whose knowledge of teaching and learning is rooted in classroom practice. His online teaching tools have been viewed and downloaded more than 3.5 million times, making them some of the most popular of all time.

He is the author of over 80 books and guides covering different areas of teaching and learning. Some of Mike's bestsellers include books on assessment for learning, questioning, differentiation and outstanding teaching, as well as Growth Mindsets. You can train online with Mike, from anywhere in the world, at www.tes.com/institute/cpd-courses-teachers.

You can also find out more at www.mikegershon.com and www.gershongrowthmindsets.com, including about Mike's inspirational in-school training and student workshops.

Training and Consultancy

Mike offers a range of training and consultancy services covering all areas of teaching and learning, raising achievement and classroom practice. Examples of recent training events include:

- Assessment for Learning: Theory and Practice Keynote Address – Leigh Academies Trust Conference, London
- Growth Mindsets: Staff Training, Student Workshops and Speech to Parents – Longton Primary School, Preston
- Effective Questioning to Raise Achievement – Shireland Collegiate Academy, Birmingham

To find out more, visit www.mikegershon.com or www.gershongrowthmindsets.com or get in touch via mike@mikegershon.com

Other Works from the Same Author

Available to buy now on Amazon:

How to use Differentiation in the Classroom: The Complete Guide

How to use Assessment for Learning in the Classroom: The Complete Guide

How to use Bloom's Taxonomy in the Classroom: The Complete Guide

How to use Questioning in the Classroom: The Complete Guide

How to use Discussion in the Classroom: The Complete Guide

How to Manage Behaviour in the Classroom: The Complete Guide

How to Teach EAL Students in the Classroom: The Complete Guide

How to be an Outstanding Trainee Teacher: The Complete Guide

More Secondary Starters and Plenaries

Secondary Starters and Plenaries: History

Teach Now! History. Becoming a Great History Teacher

The Growth Mindset Pocketbook (with Professor Barry Hymer)

The Exams, Tests and Revision Pocketbook (from April 2016)

Also available to buy now on Amazon, the entire 'Quick 50' Series:

50 Quick and Brilliant Teaching Ideas

50 Quick and Brilliant Teaching Techniques

50 Quick and Easy Lesson Activities

50 Quick Ways to Help Your Students Secure A and B Grades at GCSE

50 Quick Ways to Help Your Students Think, Learn, and Use Their Brains Brilliantly

50 Quick Ways to Motivate and Engage Your Students

50 Quick Ways to Outstanding Teaching

50 Quick Ways to Perfect Behaviour Management

50 Quick and Brilliant Teaching Games

50 Quick and Easy Ways Leaders Can Prepare for Ofsted

50 Quick and Easy Ways to Outstanding Group Work

50 Quick and Easy Ways to Prepare for Ofsted

50 Quick Ways to Stretch and Challenge More-Able Students

50 Quick Ways to Create Independent Learners

50 Quick Ways to go from Good to Outstanding

50 Quick Ways to Support Less-Able Learners

And forthcoming in Summer 2016:

50 Quick Ways to Get Past 'I Don't Know'

50 Quick Ways to Start Your Lesson with a Bang!

50 Quick Ways to Improve Literacy Across the Curriculum

50 Quick Ways to Success with Life After Levels

50 Quick Ways to Improve Feedback and Marking

About the Series

The 'Quick 50' series was born out of a desire to provide teachers with practical, tried and tested ideas, activities, strategies and techniques which would help them to teach brilliant lessons, raise achievement and engage and inspire their students.

Every title in the series distils great teaching wisdom into fifty bite-sized chunks. These are easy to digest and easy to apply – perfect for the busy teacher who wants to develop their practice and support their students.

Acknowledgements

My thanks to all the staff and students I have worked
with past and present, particularly those at Pimlico
Academy and King Edward VI School, Bury St
Edmunds. Thanks also to the teachers and teaching
assistants who have attended my training sessions
and who always offer great insights into what works
in the classroom. Finally, thanks to Gordon at Kall
Kwik for his design work and to Alison and Andy
Metcalfe for providing a space in which to write.

Table of Contents

Introduction

We all want students who are independent. Students who are prepared to work hard and pursue learning under their own steam; who don't expect everything to be handed to them on a plate; who know that spoon-feeding is neither necessary nor the best way to learn.

But how do we create these students?

Or, to put it another way, what can we do in our lessons that will foster independence? How can we plan and teach in a way that promotes self-reliance, a sense of agency and a belief that learning can be controlled and directed by students themselves?

The answer isn't easy. Nor is it straightforward. But, in this book, I'll show you fifty different techniques, ideas and approaches you can use to help achieve this important and timely goal.

Independence of mind. Independence of action. Both are habits; both aspects of character.

Any student can develop them.

They have a greater chance of doing this if their teacher is doing things, while planning, teaching and marking, which send them in this direction. Which make independence a central goal of every lesson.

Implementing some or all of the ideas which follow will take you a long way to achieving this.

So read on and enjoy – not forgetting that every entry is open to adaptation and modification. After all, you know your own students better than anybody. So you are best placed to take these ideas and tweak them to meet the specific needs of your learners.

What is independence?

01 We need to start by defining independence. Why? So that you and your students know precisely what you are talking about when you use the term. If there's a discrepancy between your definition of independence and that of your students, then you may find yourselves talking at cross-purposes without even realising it.

My definition is the following: Independence is having the ability to do things yourself, without needing help from others. An independent learner is someone who is happy to learn and work by themselves, who tries to solve problems first, before asking for help.

You might like to come up with a definition of independence with your class. This helps to bind students into the process of becoming independent.

If so, you can use this approach:

Organise the class into groups. Give each group a piece of sugar paper. Ask them to draw the outline of an imaginary student and to annotate this with all the features of an independent learner. Encourage them to give examples. Then, ask groups to come up with a one or two sentence definition summing up their diagram.

Finally, ask groups to share their definitions before asking the class as a whole to agree on a definition everybody is happy to work with.

What does independence look like?

02 Having defined independence, you now need to ensure your class know what it looks like. If they don't, it will be harder for them to work towards becoming independent learners. Here are three techniques you can use:

- Create a wall display divided into five sections: discussion; group work; individual work; start of the lesson; end of the lesson. In each section, display images, diagrams, rules, words and checklists which clearly demonstrate what independence looks like in that situation.

- Create a hand-out specifying how an independent learner would deal with different situations which commonly crop up in the classroom. For example: being unable to solve a problem; not being sure what to do next; receiving feedback from the teacher. Give students a copy of the hand-out, talk them through it and ask them to stick it in the front of their books. Refer to it through the course of the term.

- When you feel students are behaving in a highly dependent way, model alternative behaviour for them. This provides instant access to what independence looks like; and they can copy what they see.

Why does independence matter?

03 Some students may turn round and say things such as:

- I don't need to be independent now, I'll do it when I've left school.

- You're the teacher, why should we do all the work?

- What's the point of being independent when we don't get any choice about going to school?

All good questions. All understandable. All based on a certain logic.

How do we refute them, when they come? Which they inevitably will, at some point.

Reason and meaning. These are the best tools through which to convince students that independence matters.

Giving clear and unambiguous reasons means explaining to students why what you are asking them to do is important:

- Being independent now means being ready for when you move on to the next stage in your life – whether that's more education or work.

- Being an independent learner means you have a greater level of control – and that's a sign of maturity.

- Being independent is about developing a way of thinking and acting. It doesn't come overnight. You need to keep working at it. That's why we're starting now.

Coming up with responses like this in advance lets you pre-empt the kind of questions at the top of the page. You'll be well-prepared to acknowledge but then rebut any protestations students make about not wanting to be independent.

Opening Up Independence

04 Having defined independence, shown students what it looks like and rebutted any arguments against being an independent learner, our next step is to open independence up.

This means going into greater detail about what it looks like in specific situations. This is one step beyond what we examined in the second entry. We want to illustrate independence by calling on a range of examples. Here are three techniques to use:

- Start to draw the class's attention to thinking and behaviour which is indicative of independent learning. This sees you using students as models for one another.

- At the start of an activity, talk students through two or three options they could take to tackle the task independently. As you do this, praise the benefits of each approach, reinforcing it in students' minds.

- When working one-on-one with a student, talk them through how an independent learner might think in this particular situation. Then, ask them to tell you how much of this they think they could currently do, and how they are going to change their approach as a result.

Modelling Independence

05 Modelling is a powerful tool. It gives students immediate insight into other people's expertise and shows them how they might go about doing a particular thing.

You can model independence for your students in a number of ways:

- Anonymise and photocopy work which effectively demonstrates independent learning. Distribute this to students and talk them through it. Draw their attention to the different elements and encourage them to copy these in their own work.

- Show students a piece of work which demonstrates your own independence of thought and action (this could be from education, your job or your life outside work). Talk them through how you tackled this, what you did when you hit obstacles and why doing it independently led to good results.

- Create a two-part comic video with you dressed up as a student. Part one should show you playing the role of a highly dependent student – and hamming it up for comic effect. Part two should show the opposite, with you explaining how and why each decision you make is indicative of independent learning.

Step Back

06 Stepping back means passing responsibility to students. Instead of intervening at the first sign of trouble, we step back instead. This means there is an expectation on students to work things out for themselves – to be independent.

Doing this isn't always easily, not least as it goes against manty teachers' first instincts. However, here are some examples of what it looks like in practice:

- A PE teacher sets up an activity. Students are working in groups. Immediately, she sees that two groups are struggling to work out what they need to do. Instead of stepping in straight away she steels herself. In a couple of minutes the groups have got to grips with the task.

- A Year 6 teacher asks students to rewrite a piece of work using the targets he has written in their books. The class get started and two or three students look bemused. The teacher waits. After a minute or so, these students look at what their partners are doing and quickly work out what they need to do.

Refuse to Answer

6/ Refusing to answer is another way to put the onus back on the student:

- You tell me – what do you think the answer is?

- I'm not going to answer that just yet. You need to look at it again yourself.

- OK, class. For the next five minutes I won't be answering any questions. You'll need to work things out for yourself.

- You've asked me three questions there but I'll only answer one – you decide which.

- No comment. Ask me again in five minutes if you're still stuck.

If used consistently, this technique habituates students into first thinking things through themselves. Sometimes it's necessary to explicitly signal to students what you are doing (as demonstrated in the third point above); this is perhaps most true if the student in question is sensitive and may misconstrue why you are doing what you are doing.

Three Before Me

08 This means students have to do three things before they get to the fourth – asking the teacher for help. It is a technique in which you can train your students. For example, you might explain that your classroom is becoming a 'three before me' zone, where every student has to do three things before asking you for help.

When introducing the technique to your class, it is important to explain the different things which can constitute the 'three' part. These include:

- Speaking to a peer
- Using a book to look something up
- Thinking about the problem
- Using trial and error
- Using the internet for research
- Having a go and then asking a peer what they think
- Using a specific tool like a dictionary, number grid or glossary

Another tip is to make sure your classroom has books, learning tools and internet access (if possible) available, so that students have plenty of options to go through independently before asking for help.

Question Tokens

09 Give everybody in the class three tokens at the start of the lesson. Explain that whenever anybody asks you a question they will lose a token. This subtle shift in the classroom dynamic should make students think more carefully about the questions they pose and whether or not they can work out the answers themselves – or in discussion with a peer.

You can develop the technique in the following ways:

- Explain that every time a student gives up their third token, the whole class is not allowed to ask a question for the next five minutes. This changes the dynamic again, causing students to support each other by answering questions and working together.

- State which kinds of questions lose a token and which don't. For example, you might want to make it OK for students to ask questions which show independence of thought, while discouraging them from asking questions they could answer themselves.

- Instead of giving everybody three tokens, give the whole class five tokens to share. Again, this changes the dynamic and puts the onus on students to help each other out and monitor all the questions being asked.

Procedural Questions go to Peers

10 A common trait of highly-dependent students is that they ask lots of procedural questions. That is, questions about lesson procedures: how to start a task, whether they can turn over the page, and what they're supposed to be doing next.

Sometimes, procedural questions are necessary. For example, if you have delivered ambiguous instructions. Often, however, the student could work out the answer themselves and needs to get out of the habit of posing such questions without thinking.

To help them do this, make a rule that all procedural questions must go to peers – not to you. This can play out in one of two ways. First, anytime a student asks you a procedural question you throw this out to the class for somebody else to answer. Second, you appoint two or three students as procedural question-answerers. Anybody who has such a question must go to these students for help instead of coming to you.

While these techniques may not completely rid your classroom of procedural questions, they do change the focus of those questions, indicating to students that they should not be depending on you for the answer on every occasion.

Visual and Verbal Explanation

11 If students know what they need to do, it's easier for them to be independent. Similarly, if students have information to which they can refer while they are working, then they can use this to check whether they are on the right track.

Providing visual and verbal explanations achieves both these goals.

When explaining an activity to your class, ensure there is a visual explanation as well. This way, students have two types of information. They can cross-check and compare to ensure they have correctly understood what you've said.

The simplest way to do this is to always have a PPT or IWB slide containing clear guidance on what an activity entails. Another option is to use images and pictures to supplement your speech and any text you display on the board. For example, a pen to signify a writing task, or an image of a pair of scales to indicate assessment.

Finally, remember that students can assimilate visual information very quickly – more quickly than information delivered verbally. It's another reason why it always pays to use both types of explanation.

Develop Success Criteria Together

12 All tasks need success criteria. These indicate what good work looks like and give students a clear sense of what they are aiming to achieve.

Developing success criteria in conjunction with your students promotes independent learning for three reasons:

- Students feel part of the process. This empowers them to work on their own.

- Students have a better understanding of the success criteria, making it simpler for them to pursue these.

- The class as a whole have a better understanding, meaning it is easier for students to answer each other's questions.

When developing success criteria with your students, emphasise that this gives them control over a significant portion of the lesson. Highlight how this makes them more independent while also providing a basis from which they can be successful.

Independence Rules

13 Rules regulate behaviour. They can regulate the behaviour in your classroom as well. That doesn't just mean behaviour in a behaviour management sense. It also means behaviour in terms of the habits, actions and decisions students make on a daily basis.

Coming up with a set of independence rules means having a way of promoting and regulating behaviour for independent learning. Here's an example set of rules you could use:

- All students must use 'three before me' before asking the teacher for help.

- If you hit a problem, try solving it yourself first.

- When you finish your work, ask yourself what you could do next.

- If you think you have nothing to do, review your targets and try to improve your most recent piece of work.

- When you have an idea, try it out. See what happens and then tell somebody about it.

We could have a copy of these rules on our classroom wall and provide students with a version to keep in their books or on their desks. Through the year, we would keep referring to the rules, helping students to understand what they look like in practice and, eventually, to internalise them.

Question Back

14 When a student asks you a question, question them back. Here are some examples:

- **Student 1:** How do I do this, sir?
- **Teacher 1:** What ways have you tried so far? What can you think of?
- **Student 2:** Is this the right answer, miss?
- **Teacher 2:** Why do you think it might be the right answer?
- **Student 3:** What's the difference between affective and effective again, sir?
- **Teacher 3:** Why don't you tell me? What do you think the difference is?

Note how in these situations it is all about putting the explanatory effort back onto the student. It's like saying: 'I know you want to know, but I think you can come up with an answer if you try a little harder.'

It might be that, when students respond, we find out there's only so far they can go. In these cases we can give them more support, safe in the knowledge they really need it. In many case, though, you'll find students answering the question themselves and not requiring any further input.

Independence Feedback

15 You can provide students with feedback which focuses on their attempts to be independent. This has two benefits. First, it helps students to understand what they are doing well and should continue doing. Second, it gives them access to your expertise, through which they can find out what they need to do next to become more independent.

Here are two examples of independence feedback:

- Well done, Keira. I can see from your work that you've been trying various ways to solve this problem. That's good as it shows me you've been thinking carefully and using different techniques. Next time, I'd like you to stop half-way through and think about what's working, what isn't working and why. This will help you to make even better choices.

- Great job, Kyran. You decided to bowl in-swingers to the new batsman because you noticed he was uncomfortable playing off his pads. Next time I'd like you to take the lead and share what you spot with the other bowlers.

Student-Student Interactions

16 Student student interactions promote independence because the teacher ceases to be the centre of attention. Here are some ways you can promote them:

- Use group work and paired work as the basis of activities.

- Use group and paired discussions.

- Instead of posing a question to the class, taking an answer and then talking about this, pose a question to the class, take an answer and then bounce it back so that students discuss it in pairs.

- When a student asks you a question, bounce this onto one of their peers and ask them what they think.

- Before finishing an activity, give students two minutes to review their work with a partner. Provide some scaffolding by indicating key areas on which they can focus.

In each case, we are indicating to students that they are expected to lead the work. The teacher can intervene where necessary but, aside from the initial input, they have a largely facilitative role.

Admit You Don't Know

17 Sometimes students pose questions to which we don't know the answers. It could be because they've stumbled across a question we've never thought about before, because the question admits no answer, as of yet, or because we've simply forgotten all about it.

In any case, admitting you don't know is a good technique to call on. It serves to negate the idea students might have that the teacher is all-knowing. It is also another way of putting the onus back onto the student. After all, if the teacher doesn't know the answer then it is up to the student to make further enquiries or to start researching.

A fruitful avenue to follow having admitted you don't know is to work together to find an answer to the student's question. If time allows, this could happen during the lesson. If it doesn't, you and the student can agree to look into it outside of the lesson and to then bring in your findings to share and discuss.

Don't Accept First Answers

18 Often, the first answer a student gives is not their best. You can promote independence by making clear that you don't accept first answers. Instead, you always want more. This way, you are sending a message to students that they need to keep thinking even after they've shared their first thoughts.

Here are some examples of questions/statements you can use to follow up once a student has shared their first answer with you:

- OK, now can you explain that again but this time make it clearer?
- Right, show me what you mean in practice – and talk me through what you're doing as you go.
- I don't know if I can accept that answer – how can you convince me?
- Tell me again. This time, use a different example to help me understand it.
- That's an interesting angle. Why might someone disagree with you, though?
- It can take some students a while to get used to this technique. To overcome initial reticence, offer students the chance to discuss their second response with a partner before sharing it with you.

Change the Focus

19 There's nothing wrong with teacher talk. But if you use it a lot, and don't make any concessions to independent learning, then your students may become passive. Here are five techniques you can use within teacher talk to change the focus, promoting independence of thought and action:

- Provide students with three keywords or phrases. Ask them to listen out for these and to make as many notes as they can when the words/phrases come up.

- Break your talk up with opportunities for 30-second paired discussions on topics or questions connected to what you are teaching about.

- Challenge students to predict what you will talk about next, based on what you've talked about so far.

- Provide three questions before you start talking. Tell students they need to listen carefully as the answers will be contained in what you say.

- Stop talking at random points and give students three possible options for where your talk will go next. Ask them to discuss these with a partner and to predict which will come next – and to then justify their answer.

Listen

20 If you're doing all the talking in your classroom, the chances are that this will diminish the space available in which students can be independent. This often happens without the teacher realising. For example, they might reach the end of their lesson and suddenly discover they've talked so much as to dominate the majority of the session, leaving students with few opportunities to use their own initiative.

To avoid falling into this trap, focus on listening – both to yourself and to the general sounds of the classroom.

As you listen, ask yourself how dominant your voice is, and for how long.

If it feels too dominant for too long, pull back. Free up some space in which students can talk, discuss and take the lead with their work.

Then, as you continue to listen, use the opportunity to identify which students are able to do this with ease and which find it more difficult. You can then go and work with the latter, focussing your energies on helping them to be more independent.

I Won't Mark It Until...

21 You can turn this into a phrase which becomes the mantra of your classroom:

- I won't mark it until you've checked it through twice.

- I won't mark it until you've tried at least three things to improve it.

- I won't mark it until you've been through and identified the bits you think aren't right.

- I won't mark it until you've checked it for spelling, punctuation and whether or not it makes sense.

- I won't mark it until you've written me a paragraph telling me whether or not you successfully implemented your target.

In each of these examples the mantra lets students know exactly what they need to do to be independent. No longer is it a simple case of doing some work and giving it to the teacher to mark. Now they need to take more control. There are certain things they must do before they get to hand their work in. This gives them greater responsibility for their learning – at the same time as it gives them greater ownership as well.

Procedure Training

22 There are certain procedures we use again and again in the classroom. Some are about lesson practicalities:

- Giving the books out.
- Rearranging furniture for different types of activities.
- Following guidelines.
- And some are about learning:
- Checking your work before handing it in (see the previous entry).
- Using trial and error to get closer to an answer.
- Constructing paragraphs in the form of PEE – Point, Evidence, Explain.

Training students in the common procedures – practical and learning-focussed – you rely on in your classroom means giving them ways through which to be independent. Instead of shepherding, herding, reminding and cajoling students whenever they need to follow one of these procedures, you can instead rely on the fact that they have learned it off-by-heart and can get on with things themselves, without needing your support.

Procedure Practice

23 If you do decide to use procedure training (see the previous entry) it is well worth combining this with procedure practice. This involves getting students to repeatedly practice the procedure you have taught them, with the aim of being able to execute it more quickly and more proficiently.

With practical procedures like tidying the classroom or rearranging the tables this can become a game. The class's challenge is to complete the procedure as efficiently as possible. You can time them as they practice, charting their speeds and encouraging them to work together to beat their best time.

With learning-based procedures such as checking work and using trial and error, the emphasis is more on using the procedure automatically and with a high degree of skill. You can get students to practice this by asking them to do it regularly or by setting up an activity which allows them to do it repeatedly in a short space of time.

For example, you might set students five problems to solve, each of which requires the use of trial and error. When students finish a problem they move onto the next one, applying their trial and error procedures more efficiently on each occasion.

Checklists

24 Checklists overcome the limitations of memory. They expand the capacity of our minds, helping us to be more independent in the process. A common checklist many people use is: 'keys, wallet, phone.' Saying this as you leave the house, and checking each item in turn, helps overcome the propensity to forgetfulness that many people possess.

Teaching students checklists means giving them a tool on which they can rely in a wide range of situations. This makes them more independent. Here are some examples:

- **Read, annotate, reread, check**: A checklist for analysing sources in an exam.
- **Spelling, punctuation, sense**: A checklist for checking a piece of writing before handing it in.
- **Genders, tense, word order:** A checklist for checking sentences written in French.
- **Three Before Me:** A checklist for ensuring you try to solve a problem independently before going to the teacher (see earlier).
- **RAVEN:** A critical thinking checklist in the form of an acronym (Reputation; Ability to Perceive; Vested Interest; Expertise; Neutrality).

Provide Learning Tools

25 We mentioned elsewhere (Entry 8) the benefit of providing students with learning tools such as number grids, dictionaries and thesauruses. These give students something on which to call when they are uncertain or when they need a little extra help to make headway with their work.

Providing a range of learning tools means giving students a range of options when they get stuck. That means a range of ways through which to keep working independently. Here's a list of some learning tools we haven't mentioned yet:

- Crib sheets
- Exemplar work
- FAQs
- Past papers and mark-schemes
- Visual glossaries
- Mini-whiteboards, scrap paper and scrap books (all of which extend the capacity of working memory and provide a place in which students can make mistakes)
- Formulae sheets
- Instructional videos (for example, via YouTube)
- Sentence starters
- Spelling sheets

Open Questions

26 Open questions promote independence by giving students space in which to think. While closed questions are often useful (and sometimes absolutely necessary) they do tend to close thinking down and, if overused, may lead to students guessing or preferring not to answer, for fear of getting the answer wrong.

A simple way to turn any closed question into an open one is by using the word 'might':

- Why is nuclear energy not universally popular?

- Why might nuclear energy not be universally popular?

Another tip is to use a big, open question to frame the lesson or activity. You can then explain to students that it is up to them to be able to give an answer to this by the end of the lesson.

Another thing to think about is providing students with guidance on how they might go about answering an open question. We can use the example from above to demonstrate:

- Why might nuclear energy not be universally popular? In your answer, try to touch on economic factors as well as environmental ones.

Note how we give students a little bit of direction – a small scaffold, as it were – so they can concentrate on coming up with an independent answer which reflects their understanding of the matter.

Plan for Independence

27 Planning for independence means thinking in advance about when and where you will give students opportunities to lead their own learning. It means you are looking at your lesson plan through the lens of independent learning, asking yourself what you can introduce, change or tweak to give students the best chance of leading themselves.

For example, a Food Technology teacher might plan a lesson in which they take students through a recipe before letting them go off and produce their own version. Thinking about independence, the teacher could tweak their lesson plan and give students five minutes at the start of the session to look through the recipe on their own, discuss it with a partner and then bring any questions to the group as a whole.

Alternatively, a Year 5 teacher might plan a lesson on descriptive writing. The main part sees students rewriting a chunk of a recently produced story, while taking account of teacher feedback. Tweaking this lesson might involve giving students ten minutes at the start of the lesson to walk around the room and compare stories and feedback with their peers. This lets everybody develop their understanding of what good work looks like and what a rewrite could involve.

Set the Parameters

28 Sometimes less is more. Why not try promoting independence by setting the parameters for a task, but then leaving it up to your students how they respond? Here are some examples:

- Students are told they need to design an experiment which will help them to investigate friction. The teacher says they can use anything in the room in their experiment, as long as it's safe. With the parameters set, students are left to their own devices.

- An Art teacher explains they want students to produce a study of a trainer, but that their work must in some way transform the trainer. Three examples from the previous year are displayed to give students ideas. Then it's up to them.

- In an Economics lesson, the teacher tells students they need to create a presentation explaining the benefits and drawbacks of monopolies. They state that the presentation needs to include images and an interactive element but, other than this, it is for students to decide what will work best.

Provide Options and Choices

29 Another way to structure your activities so they promote independence is to make sure they include options or choices. This means students are able to take control of their learning by deciding, within the bounds you've set, what they will focus their energies on.

Here is an example:

Question: What impact does coastal erosion have on wildlife and human populations?

Choices: You can answer the question in any of the following ways – you decide:

1. Through an essay looking at the different impacts of coastal erosion.

2. With a four-part leaflet explaining what coastal erosion is, how it affects wildlife, how it affects human populations and what can be done to stop it.

3. Through a report written by an imaginary government minister who has been called to Happisburgh, Norfolk to investigate the impact of coastal erosion.

4. With a detailed plan, including key voiceover dialogue, for a television documentary looking at the effects of coastal erosion.

5. By conducting a SWOT analysis of three different attempts to halt coastal erosion. For each one, you should consider why they have been used and the extent to which they have been designed to protect wildlife, human populations or both.

Student Objectives

30 Objectives provide us with direction. This is evident in lessons, where the learning objective defines the path we and our students expect to take.

You can promote independence by asking students to set themselves independence objectives. These objectives are overarching, not just concerned with a specific lesson. It is the student's responsibility to return to their objective on a regular basis and to try to meet it through what they do in class.

Here are some examples of possible objectives (you can share these with students as a starting point):

- In team games I want to take the lead on a regular basis. I will do this by putting myself forward and giving others guidance on what they should be doing.

- When I hit a problem I want to try to solve things on my own, before asking for help. I'll do this by looking at the problem from different angles and trying out at least two different solutions.

- I want to start my work more quickly and not waste time. I'll do this by writing down my first thoughts straight away, on a piece of scrap paper, and using these to get started.

Using Technology

31 Technology opens up lots of possibilities for helping students to be more independent. Here are six techniques you can try:

1. Invite students to make revision notes using video and voice recording.

2. Set up an online forum and ask students to post links they find connected to the topic of study.

3. Let students take photographs of handouts and slides displayed on the board – they can use these as in-lesson support or when they are working at home.

4. Encourage students to make online flashcards to help them revise (for example: studyblue.com; quizlet.com).

5. Challenge students to create online revision mind-maps for each topic they study and to share these with you and the rest of the class (for example: mindmup.com; bubbl.us)

6. Divide students into groups, give each group a different topic and challenge them to create an engaging and informative Facebook page about their topic.

Question/Research

32 Research tends to involve independent learning, whether done by an individual or by a group. This is because students have something they need to find out, meaning their behaviour becomes highly goal-orientated, driving them to work things out themselves.

The most effective research tasks are framed by a research question (as opposed to a general research topic). The question serves to direct student effort more effectively because it generates additional goal-orientated behaviour (the goal is being able to give an answer, not just find something out).

Therefore, when setting up a research task, couch it in terms of a research question to gain the double benefit.

It is also worth noting that many students find a few cues helpful. For example, you might suggest some sub-questions they could begin by trying to answer, or you might indicate three key areas that provide a good starting point for their research. These techniques help students on their way, giving them scope to then branch out and become more independent in their research.

Expect More

33 What you expect from students usually determines what you get. If you expect students to be dependent, or to need spoon-feeding, then they will probably live down to this expectation. What is more, your own behaviour and the choices you make will be unwittingly shaped by this central premise.

Expecting more means expecting students to follow your lead and strive to be independent. It also means planning lessons and individual activities so that students have plenty of opportunities to be independent.

Perhaps the most important effect of expecting more, however, is that you consciously avoid planning or delivering lessons in which spoon-feeding takes place, or where students have little scope for being independent.

This might sound like an obvious point, but it demonstrates the importance of interrogating your own expectations and mindset. Ask yourself to what extent the reality of your expectations matches your desire to foster a high level of independence in your classroom.

Communicate High Expectations

34 Having established high expectations – having made sure you always expect more of your students – you should communicate this to your learners. Otherwise, how will they know?

Here are some illustrative examples:

- 'OK, Year 10. I want another independent lesson from you today. I've seen what you can do over the last few weeks and I want to see more of the same. So let's remember, that means trying to solve problems ourselves, reading ahead as soon as we finish, and not needing me to tell you to get back on track.'

- 'This is a good piece of work, Donna, but I think you can make it even better if you come up with more of your own ideas. I know you can think independently and I want to see more of that in your work. Try starting with a brainstorm before deciding which ideas are the most original – don't just go with your first one.'

- 'Well done, Sammy. I've seen the real you today – independent from start to finish. That's the standard now. That's what I know you can achieve every lesson.'

Insist on Justification

35 If a student gives you an answer, states an opinion or proposes an argument, insist on justification. Make this a rule in your classroom. Train students to understand that they will always have to justify their answers.

Why?

Because justification requires independent thinking. You need to put ideas, information and arguments together to defend whatever you've said. No one else can do this for you – you need to do it yourself.

When insisting on justification, use questions such as:

- How would you justify that?

- Can you prove what you've just said?

- Why should I believe you?

- What makes that a right answer?

- How would you explain that to me?

- What evidence do you have for that?

- Can you give me an example to prove your point?

- What if someone disagreed with you – how would you convince them you're right?

- What would need to happen for you to change your mind?

- Can you persuade me that you're right?

Project Work

36 Project work gives students space in which to develop their own ideas around a theme specified by the teacher.

Here are three examples of project work in action:

- A Maths teacher sets their students a project in which they have to develop a formula for measuring and comparing the carbon footprint of learners in their class. (For lots of Maths projects see: www.suffolkmaths.co.uk/pages/1projects.htm)

- A Geography teacher sets their students a project in which they have to assess the viability of building a new tourist attraction on the outskirts of the local town.

- A Psychology teacher sets their students a project in which they have to research the relationship between peer group proximity and adherence to group norms in teenagers of different genders.

As you can see, project work is a huge category. The one thing that runs throughout is that students are given a fairly open-ended task, limited support materials and are then left to develop the project on their own, with a partner or in teams.

It is often useful to conclude a project with a reflective activity in which students think about how they worked, what they did when they faced obstacles, and what lessons they can take away for working independently in the future.

Teach Your Parents/Carer

37 If you're teaching someone else then you are being independent. Both in thought and in action. A great homework to set students, based on this principle, is to teach their parents/carer. Here are some examples of what it can look like:

- Your homework is to teach someone at home how to factorise quadratic equations. When I see you next week I want you to tell me how you got on, what was difficult and how you overcame the obstacles.

- For your homework I want you to teach mum or dad how to write an exciting story. When I see you on Monday I want you to report back on how you taught them, what they did and whether you were successful.

- Your homework is to teach one of your parents about the basics of electromagnetism. I want you to take them through it step by step, then test them. Next lesson you'll need to tell me how you did and what their response was.

One Goal, Different Paths

38 Here's an example learning objective:

LO: To assess whether there is a moral dimension to the law

There's no reason why we couldn't anticipate different paths through which different students might achieve this objective in the same lesson. Not every student needs to achieve it in the same way.

We can share this idea with our learners, letting them know that they have a choice over how they achieve the goal. For example:

"This is our learning objective today, class. By the end of the lesson I want everybody to have achieved it. How you get there is up to you. I'll help you as we go but there's more than one way to do it."

The next step is to ensure students have different paths open to them during the lesson. In this example, we might give options such as independent research, paired analysis of key legal cases, group discussion with the teacher and so on. The point is to make it clear to students that they have a degree of agency over how they achieve the objective, with you acting as a facilitator to help them do so.

Model Metacognition

39 Metacognition means thinking about thinking. For example, I might find myself attempting to plan a lesson and notice that I keep getting stuck. On thinking about my thinking I realise that I have not broken down the lesson content. Hence, I have too much to think about. To rectify the matter I divide the content into three sections, assign each section to a portion of the lesson, and find my planning suddenly becomes much easier.

Modelling metacognition means talking students through how to think, showing them different thinking strategies, and teaching them key thinking techniques. This gives students access to your expertise in how to think – which they can internalise and use themselves, becoming more independent in the process. Here are five ways to model metacognition:

- Talk students through how to solve a problem. Narrate your thinking as you go.

- Annotate a question with your thinking. Don't give students the answer but do show them how to think about the question.

- Teach students a step-by-step process for analysis. For example, a DT teacher might teach students a step-by-step process for analysing a design brief.

- Show students memory techniques such as mnemonics and the Roman Room technique.

- In practical subjects, demonstrate a skill or piece of work while talking students through the thinking which underpins it.

Flipped Learning

40 Flipped learning is an approach to teaching that promotes independence by turning the traditional classroom setting on its head.

It tends to work in one of two ways:

1) Students engage with content outside the lesson by watching videos and reading text online. The lesson then sees the teacher facilitating group and project work in which students manipulate the content, looking at it in more depth.

2) Students engage with content inside the lesson but do this by using computers. Again, this involves watching videos, reading text and taking part in interactive activities. The teacher circulates, intervening where useful to ask questions and lead discussions. There are also structured activities and/or project work for students to complete.

The internet is awash with advice and guidance on flipped learning. If you want to find out more, visit:

- flippedlearning.org

- edutopia.org/blogs/tag/flipped-classroom

- jonbergmann.com

Why is this right?

41 Present students with an answer and ask them to tell you why it is right.

This turns the teacher-student relationship on its head. Usually it works the other way round, with the teacher telling the student why something is right. In this set-up, however, the onus is on the student to explain. This sends the message that you expect them to be independent and to work things out for themselves.

When using this technique, try to repeat it on a number of occasions over a relatively short period of time. This helps students get used to it. You may find that, at first, they are reluctant to offer an explanation. With habituation this reticence will fade.

Another way in which to use the approach is to circulate while students are working, point to something in their books or refer to something they've said and ask them to tell you why it is right. The purpose is just the same, only here the students are providing the subject matter, instead of you.

Why is this wrong?

42 This is the opposite of the previous entry.

Here we are asking students to be independent by explaining to us why something is wrong. Again, we could provide the subject matter by displaying a wrong answer or common mistake on the board, or we could use something students have said or written as the subject matter. Either way, we are asking them to take the lead.

Here is an example from a primary school numeracy lesson:

Displayed on the board:

$2 \times 10 = 12 \quad 40 + 4 = 404 \quad 10 - 2 = 5$

Teacher: Who can tell us why these are wrong? What makes these mistakes? Discuss with your partner for thirty seconds, then I'll choose some people to answer.

Each of the calculations demonstrates a common misconception or mistake. By putting the onus onto students we are asking them to take the lead on the analysis and identification of these mistakes, instead of automatically providing the answers ourselves.

Arrive With Questions

43 At the end of your lesson, spend two or three minutes outlining to students what they will be looking at next time. Then, explain you would like every student to arrive with three questions they want answered, each of which connects to the new topic.

This technique subverts the usual expectations of a lesson:

- Students arrive;

- The teacher introduces the topic;

- Students learn about the topic.

Instead, we have a different set of expectations:

- Students arrive with questions about the topic, as well as prior knowledge based on their research;

- Students share their questions with each other and the teacher;

- The lesson is driven in large part by the questions students bring.

A nice approach is to ask students to share their questions with you at the start. You can then pick out 3-5 that are either highly relevant, interesting or

which sum up the collective interests of the class. As the lesson progresses, keep returning to these questions and ask students to take the lead in assessing whether they have been answered or not.

Tell Me What to Mark and Why

44 Instead of marking every single piece of work a student produces, ask them to identify what they want you to mark – and to tell you why they want you to mark this. With this technique we are developing student independence by putting them in charge of defining what we look at. Here are some examples of how it works:

- **(Art teacher):** I want you to look back through your sketchbooks and identify the two sketches you would like me to give feedback on. When you've decided, make a note explaining why you want me to mark the ones you've chosen.

- **(Year 6 teacher):** Take a look through your personal projects. I want you to select the three pages you want me to spend the most time looking at. These are the ones I'll use to give you your feedback. Make a note telling me why these three pages are most important.

- **(Business Studies teacher):** I'm going to mark your mock exams in full, but I want you to go through and highlight the two questions you would like me to focus my feedback on. Choose the ones you found hardest or which you struggled to fully answer.

Students Setting Targets

45 When it comes to target setting, we can promote student independence by asking them to set their own targets. This isn't always appropriate as students will also need targets from the teacher, but if you can weave it into your schemes of work you should quickly see the benefits.

A useful tip is to ask students to set their own targets for individual lessons. For example, at the start of a Year 7 History lesson the teacher might ask students to look back at their earlier work, to think about what they have done well recently and what has been difficult, and to give themselves a target based on this.

Through the course of the lesson, the teacher can draw students' attention to their personal target setting and ask them to assess whether they are on course to be successful or not.

At the end of the lesson, the teacher can lead a review in which students decide if they need to keep going with the same target next lesson, or move onto something else.

Five Minute Independence Starter

46 The traditional start of a lesson runs like this:

- Students enter.

- Teacher welcomes.

- Students settle.

- Teacher displays starter on the board or explains starter verbally.

- Students get on with the starter activity.

You can subvert this, and encourage independence, by training students to do something independent at the start of your lessons, instead of a starter activity explained and presented by you. Here are some examples:

- Students start every lesson by reading through their work from last lesson and predicting what today's lesson will involve.

- Students start every lesson by swapping books with a partner and peer-assessing the work from the previous lesson.

- Students start every lesson by revisiting their current target and assessing how close they are to achieving this.

- Students start every lesson by looking up the lesson topic on their smartphones and finding out three key facts to share with their partner.

- Students start every lesson by writing out and answering a practice question based on what they learned in the previous lesson (or swapping questions with a partner and answering this instead).

You Write Your Plenary

47 At the end of the lesson, why not challenge students to write their own plenary rather than planning one yourself?

This empowers students, causing them to think carefully about their learning and how best this could be revisited/summed up/reflected on.

Initially, you will need to guide students through what a plenary aims to do. You can do this by talking them through a few different examples, drawing their attention in each case to the learning/cognitive demands they engender.

Another option is to provide students with command words they can use to shape their plenaries:

- Assess; Explain; Describe; Outline; Evaluate

Or question stems:

- What if...
- How might...
- When would...
- Why is...
- Who might...

Finally, you can develop the activity by asking students to test out their plenaries on their peers.

Students Seek Feedback

48 Teacher feedback provides students with a valuable insight into your expertise. This expertise covers subject knowledge, thinking, general cultural knowledge and much else besides.

If students start to actively seek feedback – rather than just waiting until it's given – then you know they are starting to act independently.

You can encourage this in the following ways:

- Provide a specific timeslot, outside lessons, in which students can come and see you for advice and feedback.

- Encourage students to ask you questions and to seek guidance during the lesson. You might specify certain sections of the lesson as feedback-time.

- Set up an online forum and invite students to submit posts which request feedback on specific problems or ways of working.

- Give each student in the class a feedback token and set a time limit within which the tokens need to be redeemed (three lessons, for example). Students exchange tokens for feedback, helping get them into the habit of seeking it independently.

- When students are working in groups, appoint a feedback-getter in each group. This person's role is to get useful feedback from the teacher at the most opportune moments of the lesson.

Language Change

49 Pay attention to the language you and your students use during lessons. This can reinforce or work against your aim of developing independent learners. If you or your students are using language which reinforces ideas of dependence, reframe this.

For example:

- 'I can't do this' becomes: 'You can't do it yet, but neither could I the first time I tried it. Keep practising and you'll get there.'

- 'Let me show you' becomes: 'Before I show you, what can you tell me about the problem? How have you tried to solve it so far?'

- 'I'll never get this right' becomes: 'You're not getting it right yet, but you tell me what steps you need to take to be able to do it.'

- 'Make sure you do it how I show you' becomes: 'I'll show you an effective way to do it. Copy me a couple of times so you get the hang of it, then see if you can improve the process.'

- 'Just tell me the answer, sir' becomes: 'I'll tell you the answer if you show me three things you've already done to try to work it out yourself.'

Student Leaders

50 Our final entry concerns designating certain students as leaders, either for the lesson as a whole or for individual activities. Here, we are picking out learners and conferring leadership duties on them. This turns the focus away from the teacher and onto students.

Here are some examples of how this can work:

- In a rugby lesson, the PE teacher selects three students as leaders. These learners are all skilled rugby players. They lead the rest of the group in training drills before officiating in a match at the end.

- In a literacy lesson, the teacher selects five students as leaders. These students 'captain' five groups. Each group is given a different task to complete. The teacher asks the 'captains' to lead their group in whatever task they've been given.

- In a Year 8 Citizenship lesson, the teacher appoints 4 learning leaders. These are the first port of call for any student who has a question, is unsure about something or wants advice.

And with that we draw our journey through creating independent learners to a close. Let me conclude by wishing you well in your attempts to foster a sense of agency in your classroom. By applying, adapting and modifying the techniques in this book you will be well on your way to achieving your goal.

A Brief Request

If you have found this book useful I would be delighted if you could leave a review on Amazon to let others know.

If you have any thoughts or comments, or if you have an idea for a new book in the series you would like me to write, please don't hesitate to get in touch at mike@mikegershon.com.

Finally, don't forget that you can download all my teaching and learning resources for **FREE** at www.mikegershon.com and www.gershongrowthmindsets.com

Printed in Great Britain
by Amazon